Titles in this series
Don't Call Me Special – a first look at disability
I Can Be Safe – a first look at safety
I Miss You – a first look at death
Is it Right to Fight? – a first look at conflict
My Parents Picked Me! – a first look at adoption
Stop Picking on Me – a first look at bullying
The Skin I'm In – a first look at racism

Text copyright © Pat Thomas 2000
Illustrations copyright © Lesley Harker 2000
First published by Hodder Wayland in 2000
This edition published in 2005

Reprinted in 2006 and 2007

Editor: Liz Gogerly
Concept design: Kate Buxton
Design: Jean Scott-Montcrieff

Published in Great Britain by Hodder Children's Books, a division of Hachette Children's Books

A catalogue record for this book is available from the British Library.

ISBN 978-0-340-91106-8

Printed in China

Hodder Children's Books
division of Hachette Children's Books
338 Euston Road
London NW1 3BH

I Miss You

A FIRST LOOK AT DEATH

PAT THOMAS
ILLUSTRATED BY LESLEY HARKER

Hodder
Children's
Books

Everyday someone is born...

and everyday someone dies.

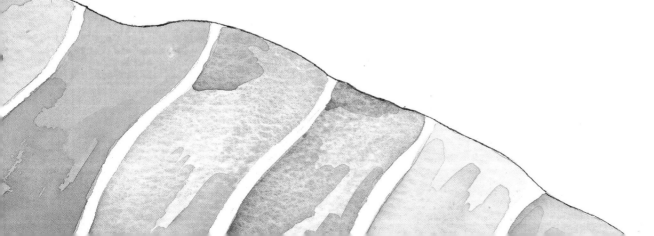

Death is a natural part of life. All living things grow, change and eventually die.

When someone dies their body stops working – they stop breathing and their heart stops beating. They can't think or feel any more. They don't eat or sleep.

In books and in films it is usually bad people who die. But in real life good people can die too.

People die for different reasons. Some people die because they are old. Some people get very sick and then they die. Some people die because something unexpected and tragic happened to them.

What about you?

Has anyone you know died? How did they die?

After a person dies there is usually a ceremony called a funeral.

At the funeral, people who knew that person can gather together to say goodbye. They may bring flowers, tell stories or recite poems.

It can be hard to say goodbye
to someone who you love.
It is normal to miss
them very much.

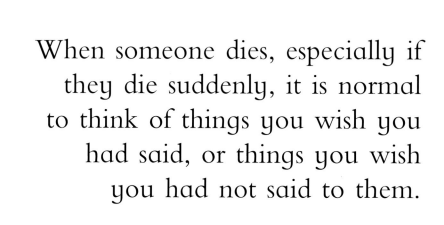

When someone dies, especially if they die suddenly, it is normal to think of things you wish you had said, or things you wish you had not said to them.

You may wish you had been nicer or
more helpful to them. But the way you
behaved did not make them die.

Try to remind yourself that they died loving you for who you were, not the things you did or said.

When someone you love dies it can feel
as if your heart has been torn in two.
It can feel as if part of you is missing.

These feelings can take a long time to get over.
You may feel lots of different sad feelings before
you finally begin to feel like yourself again.

What about you?

After someone dies it is normal to feel sad, angry,
guilty, afraid and even happy. What are you feeling?

When someone you love dies it can be hard to do
all the normal things you did before. You may
not feel like seeing your friends or joining in
groups. You may feel very alone.

Other people may find it hard to talk to you.
This is not because they don't care, but
because they don't know what to say
or do to help you.

What about you?

Have you got someone who you can talk to when you are
feeling sad? What sort of things make you feel better right now?

There is a lot we don't know about death.
Every culture has different beliefs about what
should happen after a person dies.

But most cultures also share some beliefs. Like the idea that when a person dies their soul – the part of them which made them special – takes a journey to join the souls of other people who have passed on.

It's not an easy idea to understand.

Sometimes it helps if you think of the soul like a single raindrop, joining a great big ocean.

Even after someone you know or love dies,
life goes on. The things you learned from them
stay inside of you and become a part of you.

26

As time goes on you will realize that no one is completely gone as long as you can remember them.

HOW TO USE THIS BOOK

Children need to feel that they have participated in the grieving after a death of someone close. If possible, try to encourage the child to make something for the person who has passed on which might be included in the burial ceremony. Or, if the child is old enough, let them read a poem at the funeral.

When a family member dies, it can be very difficult for all members of the family to express their feelings. Life will not be normal for many months to come. Sometimes parents get so caught up in their own grief that they forget that their children are grieving too. Try to remember that you are all in this together and that you all need each other's support. Death, especially if it is untimely, is difficult for adults to make sense of. It is even harder for children who have much less experience of the world.

If the child is your own or close to you then let them see you grieving. This is how they learn about handling grief. If they see you hiding grief away that is what they will do. If they see you allowing grief to be a part of your life, then they too will feel able to allow themselves to grieve. Allow them to mourn in your presence without having the need for it 'to make sense'. Allow them to be sad without giving in to your natural inclination to 'make it better'.

You may be the one that is grieving – for instance, if a parent has just died. Using this book can help you explain to your child how you feel. But if your child did not know the person you are grieving for very well, they may not experience the same depth of feeling. They may not feel anything at all.

Class projects about death are rare. Yet many children's lives are touched by death in one way or another. Individual children can be helped through the grieving process by being encouraged to make a special book about the person who has died. In it they can include drawings and photos. They can also record their thoughts about that person's death and their own feelings or memories. If your school is multicultural, why not get parents involved in talking about their different culture's beliefs about death? The idea is not to convince children that one belief or the other is right but to allow a subject, which is often taboo to be aired. This gives children the opportunity to think about death in a supportive space.

GLOSSARY

Funeral A ceremony in which the person who has passed on is either buried or cremated. In a burial the body is usually placed in a box called a coffin and buried in the ground. In a cremation the body is burned and the ashes are returned to the family. The family may them place the ashes in a memorial, keep them at home or scatter them somewhere special.

Soul The soul is the part of you which makes you special. You can't see the soul or touch it but everyone has one. Many cultures believe that even though the body dies the soul does not.

Grief Many people go through a period of grief after someone dies. Different people express grief in different ways. Some may feel very, very sad and tearful. Others feel tired, or lose their appetite and interest in doing things with their friends. Some feel very angry. Many people feel a mixture of these.

FURTHER READING

Fiction
Badger's Parting Gifts by Susan Varley
  (Picture Lions, 1994)
Granpa by John Burningham
  (Red Fox, 2003)
Heaven by Nicholas Allan
  (Red Fox, 2006)
Always and Forever by Alan Durant
  (Corgi Children's, 2004)

Non-fiction
Let's Talk About When a Parent Dies
  by Elizabeth Weitzman
  (Heinemann, 1998)

USEFUL ORGANIZATIONS

National Association of Bereavement Services
2nd floor
4 Pinchin Street
London E1 1SA
020 7709 9090
Can supply information on a number of NABS affiliated organizations who provide local bereavement services for children.

Childhood Bereavement Network
8 Wakley Street
London EC1V 7QE
020 7843 6309
Can provide information on local groups.

Compassionate Friends
53 North Street
Bristol BS3 1EN
08451 23 23 04
Web site: www.tcf.org.uk
Help for children who have lost family members.

Cruse Bereavement Care
Cruse House
126 Sheen Road
Richmond
Surrey TW9 1UR
020 8939 9530 (general enquiries)
0870 167 1677 (for phone counselling)
Advice, counselling and publications for anyone who has suffered a bereavement.

Child Bereavement Trust
Aston House
West Wycombe, High Wycombe
Buckinghamshire HP14 3AG
0845 357 1000
Web site: www.childbereavement.org.uk
Advice and counselling for all members of the family.